*To my daughter, Marion,
for whom the word "superstar"
is a colossal understatement.*
—K.S.

Copyright © 2025 by Katy Sprinkel

No part of this publication may be reproduced, stored in a retrieval system, or transmitted in any form by any means, electronic, mechanical, photocopying, or otherwise, without the prior written permission of the publisher, Triumph Books LLC, 814 North Franklin Street, Chicago, Illinois 60610.

Library of Congress Cataloging-in-Publication Data is available upon request.

This book is available in quantity at special discounts for your group or organization. For further information, contact:
   Triumph Books LLC
   814 North Franklin Street
   Chicago, Illinois 60610
   (312) 337-0747
   www.triumphbooks.com

Printed in U.S.A.

ISBN: 978-1-63727-845-1

Design by Patricia Frey
Edited by Laine Morreau

This book is not authorized, approved, or endorsed by Sabrina Carpenter or Island Records. It is not an official publication.

Photos on pp. 43, 44, 47, and 49 (inset, second from top) are courtesy of Photofest. All other photographs are courtesy of Getty Images.

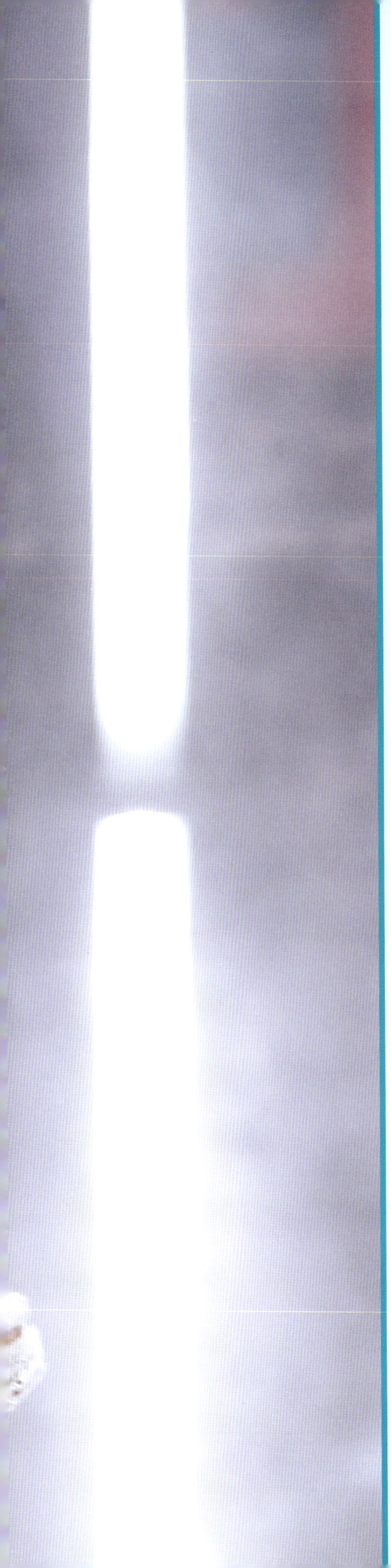

Chapter One
Short, Sweet, and on Repeat
9

Chapter Two
Little Singer Girl
19

Chapter Three
Sabrina, Meet World
31

Chapter Four
Finding Her Voice
51

Chapter Five
Breaking Through
67

Chapter Six
Born to Perform
83

Chapter Seven
All That Glitters
99

Chapter Eight
Game On
115

1

SHORT, SWEET, *and on* REPEAT

*Without question,
2024 was the **YEAR OF SABRINA**
—and 2025 is just getting better.*

Sabrina played day one of the Coachella Valley Music and Arts Festival in April 2024.

The 2024 year in music was all about the ladies. Taylor Swift was on the road night after night, celebrating her Eras. Beyoncé went country. Cool girls Billie Eilish, and Olivia Rodrigo held steady on the charts. Chappell Roan burst onto the scene. Charli XCX went full *Brat*, Tate McRae got "Greedy," and Ariana Grande got a *Wicked* boost. Yet It's hard to imagine *anyone* having a better year than Sabrina Carpenter.

From the second it began—she rang in the New Year by performing on *Dick Clark's New Year's Rockin' Eve with Ryan Seacrest*—she was on fire. Going on the road for the better part of the year, she played for fans in stadiums throughout North America, Mexico and Latin America, South America, and Asia. Then she played Coachella in April, just as she released her first single in advance of what would become her biggest album to date. She also appeared on *Saturday Night Live* in May, performing as musical guest and putting her comedic chops to the test in sketch work.

Released in August, *Short n' Sweet* was nothing short of a runaway success. It was certified platinum, selling more than 1 million albums in the United States alone. It hit No. 1 on the Billboard 200, every one of its 12 songs cracked the Hot 100 chart, and it reigned at the No. 1 spot on Billboard's Artist 100 for four straight weeks. What's more, Carpenter

SABRINA CARPENTER

scored her first career No. 1 song with "Please Please Please." The album's lead single, "Espresso," was the undisputed song of the summer—a peppy earworm that no one could shake, not that they wanted to. It became one of the biggest streaming successes of all time, breaking Spotify's all-time record for most downloads in a single month and becoming the fastest song to 1 billion streams in the history of the platform, at a brisk 146 days.

Oh, and speaking of records, Carpenter also performed on the world's most successful tour of all time, opening for none other than musical icon Taylor Swift on her Eras world tour on more than two dozen dates across four continents, ending her run in the spring of 2024. And then Sabrina went back out on the road in September, this time as headliner of her own sold-out arena tour across North America and Europe.

In November she received her first-ever Grammy nominations, scoring six nods, including the awards' highest honors: Album of the Year (*Short n' Sweet*), Record of the Year ("Espresso"), and Song of the Year ("Please Please Please"). And she closed out the year with her very own holiday variety special on Netflix, *A Nonsense Christmas with Sabrina Carpenter*, and a Tiny Desk Concert on NPR—both in December.

All in all 2024 was a whirlwind year for the 25-year-old budding superstar. And while her seemingly overnight success might feel like the splashy debut of a newly minted diva, that couldn't be further from the truth. The multitalented singer and actress has been steadily working in Hollywood for more than half her young life. This book traces her incredible journey from aspiring singer to child actress to her place today as an undisputed superstar in the making.

Strong Coffee

Caffeine isn't the only thing that's addictive. "Espresso" was Spotify's No.1 song in 2024, with the most streams of any song on the platform worldwide.

Sabrina walks the runway in the Vogue World: Paris fashion show in June 2024.

SMALL *but* MIGHTY

5'3" — Billie Eilish 5'3"

5'2" — Christina Aguilera 5'2"

5'1" — Cynthia Erivo 5'1"  Ariana Grande 5'1"

5'0" — Sabrina Carpenter 5'0"

4'11"

You know the saying: big things come in small packages. Little wonder, then, that some of the biggest voices in music come from some of the industry's most petite ladies, whose power vocals pack a serious punch.

Camila Cabello 5'2"

Shakira 5'2"

Kelly Clarkson 5'1"

Lady Gaga 5'1"

Dolly Parton 5'0"

Kristin Chenoweth 4'11"

"I'm struggling to find the words to express just how magical the last 365 days with each other have been.... Putting out the album was one thing... but the way you guys gave it such incredible life was another.... Childhood dreams coming true all because of you guys. I can't thank you enough."

—Sabrina, reflecting to fans via email at the end of 2024

2

little SINGER GIRL

*A **STRONG FAMILY** support system set the stage for **FUTURE SUCCESS**.*

Sabrina, Zachary Gordon, and Sabrina's sisters Sarah and Shannon attend Gordon's 16th birthday party in 2014.

Sabrina Annlynn Carpenter entered the world on May 11, 1999, to parents David and Elizabeth. She is the youngest of four girls, following half-sister Cayla (eight years her senior) and sisters Shannon (five years older) and Sarah (three years older).

Born in Quakertown, Pennsylvania, Sabrina grew up in nearby East Greenville, a small community of just a few thousand residents. While just 30 minutes from Allentown and an hour from Philadelphia, East Greenville felt worlds away from the cities' hustle and bustle. Sabrina remembers the peace of being surrounded by trees, nature giving space to her thoughts. To this day, her mother encourages her to go put her feet in the grass, wherever she might be, to find her inner calm.

Her parents homeschooled her and her sisters, and the Carpenters were a tight family unit. Reflecting on her childhood to *People*, Sabrina recalled, "[My parents] were very, very kind and supportive. I always remember that." They encouraged her to follow her creative passions, enrolling her in dance classes starting at age two. (Her mother had been a professional dancer as a young woman.) Young Sabrina also took music lessons, including piano and voice. She soon gave up on piano lessons when she realized she wasn't

SABRINA CARPENTER

With Paul McCartney at the MusiCares gala in 2024.

learning the type of music she wanted to—"I didn't want to have to learn 'Alouette,'" she told *Rolling Stone*—instead turning to YouTube tutorials on guitar and piano.

Sabrina's story starts the same way a lot of famous musicians' do: in a house filled with music. "My parents introduced me to such a range of music...at such a young age," she told Zane Lowe in a 2024 Apple Music interview. There was always a steady diet of '70s tunes humming, from disco titans such as the Bee Gees and ABBA to easy listening like the brother-and-sister act the Carpenters. On top of that, she was also raised on inimitable ladies from Etta James to Judy Garland to Dolly Parton.

Yet of all the musical inputs Sabrina received early on, the Beatles reign supreme. Sabrina has often said that her favorite album of all time is the group's *White Album* (the official title of which is simply *The Beatles*). And if there's one person who has singularly influenced Sabrina's songwriting, it's Paul McCartney.

She remembers hearing "Rocky Raccoon" for the first time and feeling like she'd been hit by a thunderbolt. "I remember [my dad] turning on this song, and immediately I was like, 'This is music?'.... There is such a story behind it and...all their songs, and it made me

No Nonsense

really want to be a songwriter," she told *Teen Vogue* in 2018.

It was the first time Sabrina really understood that the power of a song could be completely transformative. "I was so mesmerized by the song and the songwriting of it that I fell in love with Paul McCartney. I was convinced that was my...future husband," she told *The Late Show with Stephen Colbert*. (As luck would have it, she did cross paths with Paul McCartney in the future. And though she no longer confused musical love with romantic love, she was still rendered speechless when they met at a charity gala in February 2024.)

Also, like most little girls, Sabrina was influenced by the contemporary artists she heard on the radio. "All of the posters on my wall were women," she told Lynn Hirschberg in a 2024 video interview. "Miley Cyrus, Taylor Swift, Ariana Grande."

The Little Singer Girl, as she was affectionately nicknamed by those who knew her, found opportunities to entertain wherever and whenever. She just *needed* to sing. "I can't even remember when I started singing and performing and entertaining, because I was really, really little," she told *W* magazine.

Sabrina remembers something really clicking when she got on the mic at age

COVER STORY

Sabrina posted her first YouTube video in August 2009, when she was just 10 years old. It was a cover of Taylor Swift's defiant breakup song "Picture to Burn," from her self-titled debut album. Fourteen years later, the two singers would share the stage on Swift's Eras tour.

eight at a family gathering. "Everyone just had way too much alcohol, so they were so fascinated by this little eight-year-old singing karaoke," she told JJ Ryan in a radio interview. In truth, her family was gobsmacked, and they all agreed she had what it took to make it big.

A strong female role model, Sabrina's mom, Elizabeth, is a chiropractor with her own practice. Her dad, David, is a skilled contractor. When Sabrina

SABRINA CARPENTER

was young, he built a makeshift recording studio for her in a closet in the family's home. It was there that she recorded her first YouTube videos. "I was in this purple phase, 'cause all the girls at school really liked purple," she said in an interview with Urban Outfitters in 2019. "He painted my entire studio purple and put the foam walls up for me."

Sabrina's home studio was also a safe place where she began to hone her songwriting skills. "That's where I really found comfort in creative space," she told *Marie Claire* magazine.

It was in that little room where Sabrina's dream of becoming a singer truly took wing. She started posting videos of herself singing covers (and, eventually, some original compositions) when she was just 10 years old. She was particularly attracted to songs by her contemporary role models at the time, including Miley Cyrus, Adele, and Taylor Swift.

> "I knew this is where I'd end up. I was that kid who dreamed about it, but I knew it wasn't always going to be just a dream."
>
> —Sabrina to *Vanity Fair*

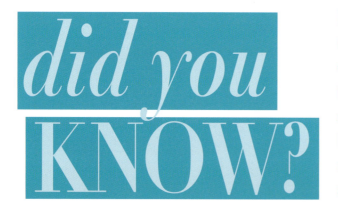

Bethlehem, Pennsylvania, holds a multiday event called Musikfest each year. The largest free music festival in the country, it was a can't-miss event for the music-loving Carpenter family. In a full-circle moment, Sabrina headlined one day of the event in 2016!

Sabrina and Sarah in 2014.

SABRINA CARPENTER

It's a family affair as parents David and Elizabeth, along with sister Shannon, help Sabrina launch her album Eyes Wide Open *in 2015.*

In 2009, when Sabrina was 10 years old, she entered a singing contest called the Next Miley Cyrus Project, which was run by Cyrus, the child actor–turned–recording superstar. Entrants were asked to submit videos for the contest to Cyrus's fan site. Sabrina covered artists as wide-ranging as Michael Jackson, the Beatles, and Christina Aguilera in her videos, beating out thousands of entrants and finishing third overall.

Having made an impressive showing and turned the heads of executives at Disney, Cyrus's home, the writing was on the wall: bigger things awaited. Ultimately, the Carpenter family decided to uproot and move to Los Angeles in pursuit of turning their daughter's dream into a reality, and when Sabrina was 13 years old, the Carpenters ultimately chose to make the big move out West.

SISTER
act

Anyone plugged in to Sabrina's socials knows how close she is with her three siblings; the four of them are a mutual-admiration society unto themselves. They often post on their respective social media channels with snapshots of themselves together and messages in support of their respective endeavors. Creativity runs in the family, as all four of the girls have gone on to pursue artistic endeavors in their careers. Cayla is a hairstylist and makeup artist, Shannon is a dancer, and Sarah is a creative director who has worked behind the scenes on many of Sabrina's projects.

¡Ay Caramba!

While Sabrina grew up in rural Pennsylvania, she has a very famous relative from the town of Springfield: Bart Simpson!

Nancy Cartwright, Sabrina's aunt (father David's sister), has voiced the famous fourth grader since 1987. (She's also the voice of many other iconic characters on *The Simpsons*, including Ralph Wiggum, Nelson Muntz, and Todd Flanders.) A prolific voice actress, the Emmy-winning Cartwright has voiced animated characters in dozens of other series, including *Animaniacs*, *Kim Possible*, and *Rugrats*.

Sabrina has undoubtedly picked up some showbiz pointers from her famous aunt. "We work in different sides of the industry, (but) I've learned so much just from observing her. She's so talented," she told *Wired* in a 2021 interview.

That feeling is mutual. Talking to *Good Morning America* about her famous niece in 2024, Cartwright said, "(Stardom) was her dream at age six. She has just created her own path…. I wouldn't be surprised if she has an EGOT someday."

EGOT It?

Coined by *Miami Vice* actor Philip Michael Thomas in 1984 and popularized by the sitcom *30 Rock*, the term EGOT describes a multitalented entertainer who has won at least one Emmy, Grammy, Oscar, and Tony Award. To date, there are only 21 EGOT winners in history. Sabrina told *Teen Vogue* in 2020 that she had her sights set on joining that lofty company someday.

Attending the Happy Feet Two premiere with her famous aunt in 2011.

3

SABRINA, meet WORLD

*Disney provided **SABRINA** with her first big acting break.* ***THE REST IS HISTORY.***

Sabrina's Girl Meets World *castmates were like a second family.*

After her success in Miley Cyrus's singing competition, Sabrina's dreams of making it in the entertainment industry were soaring, and she set her sights on Hollywood. As a young person trying to break into what is a notoriously difficult industry, she pondered whether singing or acting was the right way to begin a lasting career.

She, her family, and her agent suggested that she might have better luck getting a foot in the door as a young actress, since there were many more opportunities for youngsters in that field. Speaking to *Time* in 2024, Sabrina said, "I knew that I wouldn't be able to thrive as a recording artist the same way I would have been able to working on a show as a child actor—which I know sounds weird to have that perspective at 12, but I was really lucky to."

The bubbly, confident youngster was up for the challenge, and started going out on auditions. She booked her first gig at age 11, playing a victim on the crime procedural *Law & Order: Special Victims Unit*. "It was so dramatic and scary," she told *NME*, and she felt like she was getting thrown into the deep end by landing on such an established production in her first role. It was intimidating but exhilarating, and just like that, she was hooked. Her next role was in Netflix's prison drama *Orange Is the New Black*, starring in a very NSFW-titled episode of the show.

Happily, lighter fare soon followed. She was booked in a variety of supporting roles in TV and feature work, and even voice work as the character Princess Vivian on the Disney animated series *Sofia the First*, a role that spanned multiple seasons in the show's run. "I went from raunchy to Disney," Sabrina quipped to *W* magazine in 2024.

She appeared poised for something big when she was cast as a regular alongside Scott Foley, T. J. Miller, and Becki Newton on *The Goodwin Games*, a network sitcom centering around three siblings who compete to win a rather sizeable family inheritance. But the series was canceled after seven episodes.

It was a disappointment, but the role that would change the whole trajectory of her acting career was just around the corner. At age 13 she landed her first steady job when she was cast as a series regular on *Girl Meets World*, a role that would catapult her onto the national stage. With Sabrina's acting career taking off and steady work rolling in, the Carpenter family finally made the decision to leave Pennsylvania for Los Angeles permanently.

A reboot of the '90s sitcom *Boy Meets World*, *Girl* picks up a generation later. Cory and Topanga have married and now have children of their own: daughter Riley and son Auggie. Sabrina plays Maya Hart, Riley's best friend. The show called for lots of broad comedy—pranks, hijinks, and general fun— and Maya (like her *Boy Meets World* corollary Shawn) is the prankster-in-chief, always leading the steadier Riley into the sort of pratfalls and sticky situations so common in sitcoms. Yet Maya is a character with an uncharacteristic depth for the medium. Raised in a single-parent household, she struggles with issues surrounding her absent father. She has a magnetic personality due to her outward

> "[Acting] is an incredible way to reach so many people of all different ages."
> —Sabrina to *PeopleNow* on her *Girl Meets World* fan base

Sabrina first caught the attention of entertainment execs after participating in an online singing contest hosted by Miley Cyrus.

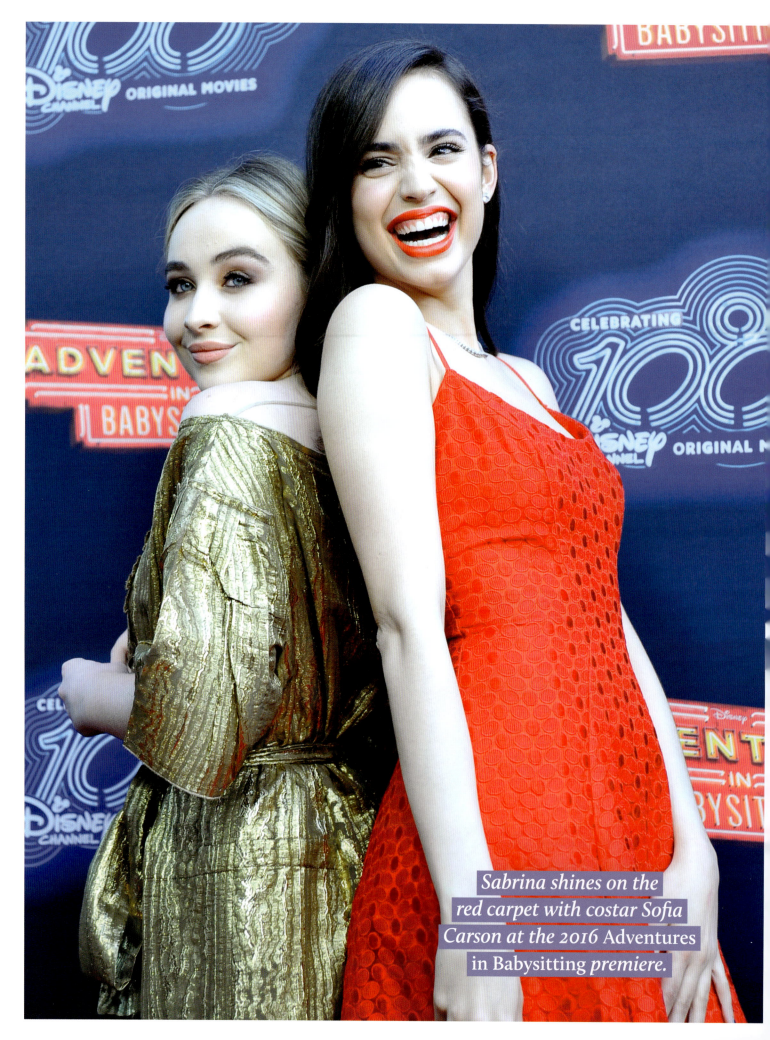

Sabrina shines on the red carpet with costar Sofia Carson at the 2016 Adventures in Babysitting premiere.

No Nonsense

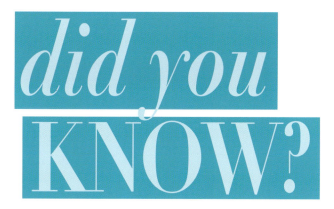

Sabrina's first TV appearance was actually in China, at age nine. One of her YouTube posts went viral there, and she was invited to sing at a Hunan TV festival, where she covered a Christina Aguilera song.

confidence but also craves stability, which she gets from the Matthews family.

Sabrina's run on the show from 2014 to 2017 also coincided with some pretty vital years in her adolescence. "That was my childhood in every way, shape, and form," she said on the *Chicks in the Office* podcast in 2020. "I grew up on that set. I grew up around those people, and luckily they were very kindhearted, intelligent people that definitely gave me the ability to experiment. And I definitely credit a lot of what I do now and where I am [to] that show and that character I got to play. So yeah, [it was] a very, very special project."

After the series wrapped, Sabrina went on to star in a variety of other productions on the Disney Channel. She played the lead character in the remake of *Adventures in Babysitting*, opposite another rising Disney star in Sofia Carson. She lent her considerable voice talents to the animated series *Milo Murphy's Law*. And in the teen drama *Clouds*, she played the best friend of a boy who copes with a cancer diagnosis by pursuing his dreams of becoming a musician.

She also recorded numerous songs during her stint at Disney. She performed songs for nearly all the shows she appeared in—including the theme song to *Girl Meets World*, which she sings with her on-screen cohort Rowan Blanchard; "Wildside" and "We're the Babysitters," both with Carson, from *Adventures in Babysitting*; and the beautiful duet "Clouds" with Fin Argus from the movie of the same name. Her songs were also used for other Disney projects, including *Disney Fairies* and *How to Build a Better Boy*.

SABRINA CARPENTER

> "I'm 900 inappropriate jokes away from being a Disney actor, but people still see me that way.... [But] I'm always extremely flattered to be grouped in with the other women and girls who I've idolized and looked up to who came from that."
>
> —Sabrina to *Variety*

Her good fortune to start her career with the multimedia juggernaut Disney was an invaluable opportunity, one she has never taken for granted. And she credits that work as building a solid foundation for the rest of her career. "Any performer that has come from [Disney] and has had the opportunity to grow and become the artist they are now knows how hard it is, and how tricky it can be. A lot of people have preconceived notions of [child stars], but so many of them are still successful today," she told Bustle in 2022.

The opportunities kept coming for Sabrina, and she worked steadily through her late teens and early twenties, scoring big roles in Netflix projects *Work It* and the *Tall Girl* films, among other projects.

And fulfilling a bucket list item, she appeared on *Saturday Night Live* in 2024, reacting via Instagram, "I'm sooooo not chill about it and never will be." Though invited as a musical guest, Sabrina's obvious skill set for comedy made her a shoo-in for sketch work, and she appeared alongside host Jake Gyllenhaal in a sketch lampooning *Scooby-Doo*. The hilarious spoof went viral and has more than 4 million views on YouTube as of this writing.

With Sabrina's music career going full steam ahead these days, acting has taken a backburner...for now. But it's only a matter of time before we see her back on the big screen. (Perhaps Sabrina's *Alice in Wonderland* project will get off the ground, for one; she sold rights to a musical adaptation of the Lewis Carroll novel *Alice's Adventures in Wonderland* to Netflix in 2020.)

Have you seen all of Sabrina's greatest hits? From serious dramas to sitcoms to animated series, the girl has covered a lot of ground. (I mean, she even appeared in the video game *Just Dance Kids 2*—a deep cut for the die-hard fans!) Here's a rundown of some of her most notable acting roles so far.

Appearing at Nickelodeon's SlimeFest in 2014.

Disney kids Sabrina and Rowan Blanchard in 2014.

the WONDERFUL world of DISNEY

The House of Mouse has launched the careers of innumerable stars. Here are just a few of the many award-winning actors and musicians who got their start at Disney. Britney Spears, Christina Aguilera, Ryan Gosling, Keri Russell, and Justin Timberlake were all Mouseketeers in the late 1980s and early '90s. Miley Cyrus, the Jonas Brothers, Selena Gomez, Hilary Duff, and Zendaya all had their own shows. Zac Efron and Vanessa Hudgens got their big break on *High School Musical*, and Olivia Rodrigo shined on *High School Musical: The Musical: The Series* a decade later. Lindsay Lohan, Demi Lovato, Dove Cameron, Raven-Symoné, Dylan and Cole Sprouse…heck, even Kurt Russell—the list goes on and on!

GIRL meets WORLD

72 episodes; 2014-17

THE PREMISE: A spinoff of the popular *Boy Meets World*, the show follows the life of teenager Riley Matthews, the daughter of couple Topanga and Cory from the original series.

THE CHARACTER: Maya Hart, Riley's best friend. Maya has had a difficult childhood, which sometimes leads her to rebellious behavior. Creative, confident, and unflinchingly loyal to her BFF, she is an unofficial member of the Matthews family.

CLASSIC LINE: "You're my favorite person in the world. I wouldn't change a thing about you." BFF goals!

FUN FACT: Sabrina was originally cast to play Riley, and Rowan Blanchard was set to play Maya!

ADVENTURES in BABYSITTING

2016

THE PREMISE: A reimagining of the 1987 movie of the same name, it follows two babysitting gigs gone terribly wrong and explores the misadventures that bond the group—two babysitters and their respective charges—firmly together.

THE ROLE: Jenny Parker, a straitlaced, uber-responsible babysitter who must save her own babysitting reputation and keep two families' kids safe—and get them home before their parents find out they're gone!

CLASSIC LINE: "Don't mess with the babysitter!"

FUN FACT: The remake contains several nods to the original feature, including Jenny's camel-colored overcoat and a scene in which the characters must perform an impromptu musical number.

Maya and Riley get lunch lady duty on Girl Meets World.

With Amandla Stenberg in The Hate U Give.

the HATE U *give*

2018

THE PREMISE: Based on the novel of the same name, it is a meditation on gun violence, race, and the ties that bind. The film follows 16-year-old Starr as she code-switches between two different worlds and navigates life after tragedy.

THE CHARACTER: Hailey, a sheltered prep school student and classmate of Starr's.

CLASSIC LINE: "So I guess you're not going to get over it anytime soon."

FUN FACT: According to author Angie Thomas, the title comes from a quote by the late rapper/activist Tupac Shakur, and the main character's name was inspired by Shakur's love of the Vincent van Gogh painting *The Starry Night*.

the SHORT HISTORY *of the* LONG ROAD

2019

THE PREMISE: Nola and her father live a nomadic life, traveling the country in a battered RV. When tragedy strikes, Nola is forced to confront a new reality, leading her to make unlikely connections outside of her family unit.

THE CHARACTER: Teenager Nola has never known "normal." Fiercely independent, she navigates grief, financial insecurity, and uncertainty, ultimately finding a way to trust in others.

CLASSIC LINE: "Not everyone wants to live like us."

FUN FACT: Sabrina went brunette to play Nola in the movie.

tall GIRL and *tall* GIRL 2

2019; 2022

THE PREMISE: Jodi Kreyman is just your average high schooler, but her 6'1" height leads her to grapple with her own insecurities.

THE CHARACTER: Harper Kreyman is petite, blonde, beautiful, and accomplished. A pageant queen and the apple of her parents' eye, she is everything her sister, Jodi, is not—at least in Jodi's eyes.

CLASSIC LINE: "There's no worse bully than the one you create inside your own head." Now *that's* sisterly advice!

FUN FACT: Sabrina dated costar Griffin Gluck IRL. He played her on-screen sister's lovestruck best friend.

WORK *it*

2020

THE PREMISE: In a desperate bid to get into Duke, a high school student forms a dance team to impress a college admissions counselor. To achieve it, she assembles a ragtag group of disparate dancers. There's only one hitch: she's never danced before.

THE CHARACTER: Quinn Ackerman is a good student, driven and focused on her goals. She and her best friend, Jasmine, are sister-close, despite being very different.

CLASSIC LINE: "Albert Einstein once said, 'Dancers are the athletes of God.' Kim Kardashian once said, 'Lighting is everything.' And, as head of the AV club, I had to agree."

FUN FACT: Sabrina and costar Liza Koshy, the hilarious YouTuber, became fast friends while shooting the movie. "We grew so close, it was like the summer camp of our dreams," Sabrina said in a 2020 interview.

Finding her groove with costar Jordan Fisher in Work It.

QUIZ
Which Sabrina character are you?

1. You have to give a speech in school today. How are you feeling?
   A. That was today? Guess I'm pulling the fire alarm.
   B. Prepared but nervous. Public speaking isn't really my thing.
   C. Confident! I thrive in front of an audience.
   D. Petrified! Can I have the bathroom pass, please?

2. Oh no, you're grounded, and it's Friday night. You:
   A. Sneak out of the house once your parents are asleep.
   B. Stay in and work on your homework.
   C. Text all your friends at the party and tell them you wish you could be there.
   D. Dig back into your book. You weren't planning on going out anyway.

3. I couldn't live without my:
   A. Sketchbook.
   B. Day planner.
   C. Lipstick.
   D. Pet.

4. Describe your friend group.
   A. A tight-knit group of girls and guys.
   B. My BFF and I are like sisters.
   C. Everyone I meet is a friend.
   D. I mostly keep to myself.

5. My idea of a perfect Saturday is…
   A. Going on an elaborate adventure.
   B. Catching up on my chores, curling up with a good book in the afternoon, then meeting up with my BFF at the movies.
   C. Date night, obvi.
   D. Playing music or taking a long walk.

6. My favorite subject in school is:
   A. Art.
   B. Drama. (I'm on tech crew!)
   C. Speech.
   D. Music.

7. My Achilles' heel is:
   A. My temper.
   B. My ambition.
   C. My allergies.
   D. My self-consciousness.

8. Finish this sentence: I dance…
   A. Like no one is watching.
   B. With my head, not my heart.
   C. To win.
   D. Only when I can't avoid it.

9. If I were an element, I would be:
   A. Fire.
   B. Earth.
   C. Air.
   D. Water.

Mostly A's: Maya Hart (*Girl Meets World*)
You're a super-creative soul with a little bit of a wild streak. A true-blue friend, that's what your besties love most about you. You're always up for something new—and it's usually your idea!

Mostly B's: Quinn Ackerman (*Work It*)
You're driven, organized, and risk-averse. Change can be hard for you, but you're working on it. (Get it?!) You and your bestie are inseparable, and you bring out the best in one another.

Mostly C's: Harper Kreyman (*Tall Girl* and *Tall Girl 2*)
You're kind, well-liked, and popular. And you also work hard for the things that are important to you; whether it's being a great sister or winning honors in your chosen pursuit, you always give it 100 percent.

Mostly Ds: Princess Vivian (*Sofia the First*)
You're shy, so it takes you longer to get to know people. But once you do, you're bonded for life! You're comfortable hanging in the background and letting others have the spotlight.

4

FINDING *her* VOICE

Sabrina started her musical career early, **RELEASING HER FIRST RECORD** *when she was just* **15 YEARS OLD.**

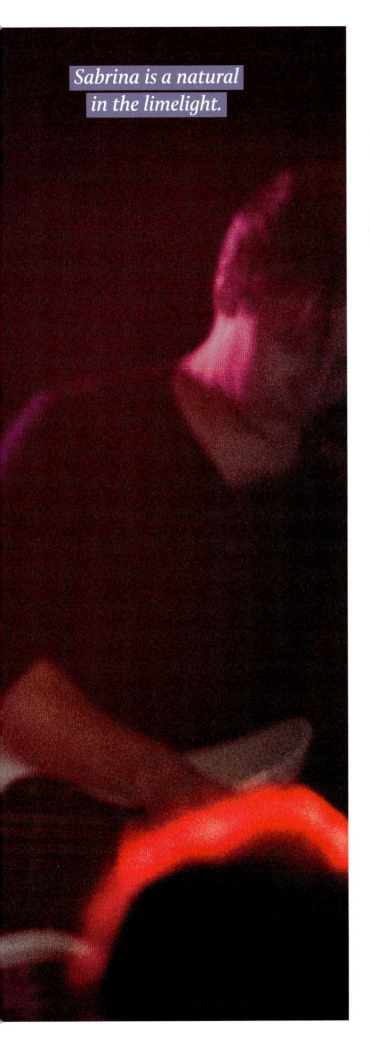

Sabrina is a natural in the limelight.

Sabrina may have been elevated to the national stage as an actress on *Girl Meets World*, but she also reached a major milestone in her career shortly before landing the role when she signed her first record deal with Disney's Hollywood Records at age 12. The youngster turned heads there after her showing in the Next Miley Cyrus Project contest, and executives felt she had something special. Indeed, the five-record deal underscored the belief that Disney had in the emerging star, as she was tabbed to be a multihyphenate in the mold of Selena Gomez, Demi Lovato, and, yes, Cyrus herself.

To get her feet wet, Sabrina recorded several songs for Disney straight out of the gates, including a number of musical performances in-episode for *Sofia the First* (most notably "All You Need") as well as the song "Smile," which appeared on the *Disney Fairies: Faith, Trust and Pixie Dust* soundtrack.

Then, to launch their pop star in the making, Disney enlisted a talent known for her catchy hooks and bubble gum–sweet lyrics: performer and songwriter Meghan Trainor, fresh off her own breakthrough debut. Trainor worked with Sabrina to launch her debut single, "Can't Blame a Girl for Trying." The stripped-down song has the bouncy, acoustic feel of Colbie Caillat and Jason

SABRINA CARPENTER

*'Cause I'm young, and I'm dumb.
I do stupid things for love.
And even if I always end up crying,
no, you can't blame a girl for trying.*

Mraz. It's a perfect showcase for what was then Sabrina's already-powerful voice, as the song vacillates between the hopefulness of finding love and the disappointment of losing it. The song was launched on the Disney Channel and was also included as part of a four-song EP by the same name.

Ahead of the launch, Sabrina spoke to Radio Disney about the single's relatability and the universality of its themes. "It's about failure and messing up and just being yourself and…embracing who you are and not being afraid to show yourself." It was promoted heavily on the Disney Channel and Radio Disney, and in conjunction with the popularity of *Girl Meets World*, Sabrina quickly became a familiar face to audiences at the network.

With a successful rollout of the EP complete, it was time to release a full album. The following pages look at all of Sabrina's work with Hollywood Records, beginning with her freshman record, *Eyes Wide Open*.

> "The way that I think about music and when I'm releasing music, it's great that I can write songs that are for me, that [fans are] supportive of. But then, a lot of these songs are for them. I want to support them and what they're going through—and let them know that we're going through it together at the same time."

—Sabrina to PopCrush

Sabrina commands the stage at the famous Roxy in Los Angeles in 2016.

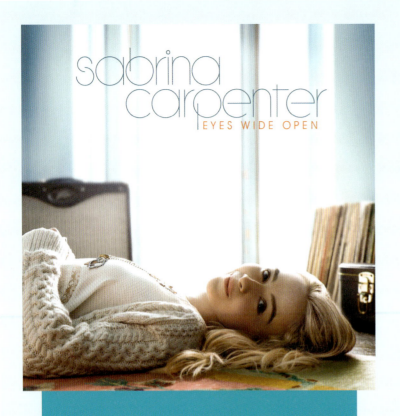

EYES wide OPEN

Track List:

1. Eyes Wide Open
2. Can't Blame a Girl for Trying
3. The Middle of Starting Over
4. We'll Be the Stars
5. Two Young Hearts
6. Your Love's Like
7. Too Young
8. Seamless
9. Right Now
10. Darling I'm a Mess
11. White Flag
12. Best Thing I Got

The record includes all four singles from the EP *Can't Blame a Girl for Trying*, and an additional track penned by Trainor: the pert "Darling I'm a Mess."

Released on April 14, 2015, Sabrina's debut full-length album covered a lot of ground. At least some of that is due to the fact that it was written and recorded over a three-year period, an unusually long time for development. "It's so funny because I started writing this album when I was 13 but produced it when I was 16," she said in a 2017 interview. "So [in]...that time, there was already a huge change."

The songs express all the bottled-up emotions of a typical teenager—the ups and downs of young love, the uncertainties and anxieties of growing up, and the spirit of youthful optimism. Inflected with pop, folk, and a little bit of country, it is a solid first effort from a young artist just starting to make her mark.

THE VIBE: Plucky, folky, and brimming with youthful exuberance, *Eyes Wide Open* also echoes the pop-country stylings popularized by Taylor Swift on her early albums.

CRITICAL RECEPTION: "She might be astute, mature, and in possession of immense talent, but her greatest asset is her refusal to run from her youthful self. She refuses to be anyone but a teenager with a pretty voice and real feelings…. She is not simply performing her songs but living them and feeling them. Carpenter is a great artist in the making."—Headline Planet

> *This dream burns inside of me*
> *And I can't just let it go.*

WHEN YOU'RE UP: "We'll Be the Stars" is squarely a ballad, but the message will have you hyped!

WHEN YOU'RE DOWN: "Can't Blame a Girl for Trying" captures the heartbreak of young love, and the thrill of finding it once again.

spotlight on
MEGHAN TRAINOR

There's no "treble" figuring out why Disney tapped Trainor to cowrite on Sabrina's debut. The singer-songwriter had already hit pay dirt with "All About that Bass," her 2014 coming-out party and single that was fizzy, fun, and girly—attributes befitting Sabrina's debut as well. Trainor cowrote two songs on Sabrina's first record, providing some of its lightest fare.

Trainor, known for her throwback sound, has continued to forge a successful career as a recording artist, including recent hits such as "Made You Look." But her behind-the-scenes work as a songwriter has been just as impressive. She's penned hits for artists as diverse as Jennifer Lopez ("Ain't Your Mama"), Michael Bublé ("Someday"), and Rascal Flatts ("I Like the Sound of That"), and has cowritten with the likes of John Legend, Harry Styles, and Fifth Harmony.

EVOLution

Track List:

1. On Purpose
2. Feels Like Loneliness
3. Thumbs
4. No Words
5. Run and Hide
6. Mirage
7. Don't Want It Back
8. Shadows
9. Space
10. All We Have Is Love

Released on October 14, 2016, *EVOLution* was a big shift for Sabrina stylewise, as she stepped away from the country- and folk-tinged strains of her freshman album and took her music onto the dance floor. The vocals retained the confessional style of her previous work, but sonically they had more in common with the pop divas of the day, including Rihanna and Ariana Grande. It didn't go unnoticed; Grande asked Sabrina to join her on her Dangerous Woman tour later that year.

Sabrina launched her sophomore album with the catchy "On Purpose," a soul sister to Natasha Bedingfield's "Unwritten" and Taylor Swift's *1989*. Her second single was "Thumbs," a meticulously crafted jazz-inflected single and the biggest standout on the record. A rejection of banality, it became her first Top 40 hit, and in April 2017 she notched another first, performing the song on *The Late Late Show with James Corden*, her first-ever late-night appearance.

THE VIBE: The perfect record to put on while you're getting ready for a Friday night out.

CRITICAL RECEPTION: "At 17 years old [she] is dominating all things entertainment...a phenomenal artist.... *EVOLution*...embraces its meaning and purpose—change. With each track we get to hear how Sabrina's voice has grown since the release of *Eyes Wide Open* last year.... Obsessed."—*Girls' Life* magazine

> *Don't just march to the beat of that drum*
> *Don't be one of them people just twiddlin' them thumbs*

WHEN YOU'RE UP: The super-danceable "Space" is an ode to self-agency that connected with fans from the jump.

WHEN YOU'RE DOWN: The anthemic "All We Have Is Love" is a bop in the vein of Ariana Grande's "No Tears Left to Cry" that'll have you dancing through the hard times.

spotlight on STEVE MAC

Sabrina worked with a number of heavy hitters on her sophomore album, including producers Daylight, Halatrax, and Ido Zmishlany, and British DJ and musician Steve Mac. Mac worked with Sabrina to cowrite arguably the biggest hit on the record, the bouncy and lyrically dense "Thumbs."

Born Steve McCutcheon, Mac started his career as a producer in the UK, working with dance groups including Nomad, Westlife, and his own Undercover. Over the years he's collaborated with some of the biggest names in music in Britain and abroad, working with artists across a wide spectrum of musical genres, from DJ Calvin Harris to singer-songwriter James Blunt and even reality star–turned-diva Susan Boyle. Among his many monster hits are Clean Bandit's "Rockabye" (feat. Sean Paul), The Wanted's "Glad You Came," and Ed Sheeran's "Shape of You." Mac is a Grammy Award winner many times over, and in addition, in 2017 the American Society of Composers, Authors, and Publishers (ASCAP) awarded him its Founders Award for his "pioneering contribution to music, global success, and a 27-year body of work."

SINGULAR act I

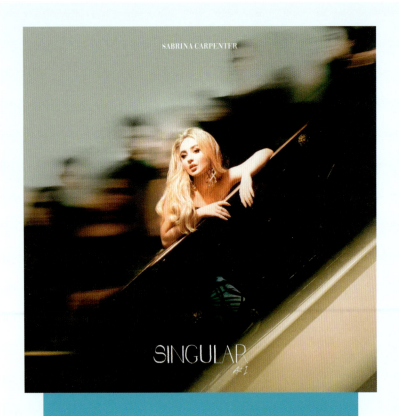

Track List:

1. Almost Love
2. Paris
3. Hold Tight
4. Sue Me
5. Prfct
6. Bad Time
7. Mona Lisa
8. Diamonds Are Forever

After wrapping *Girl Meets World* and embarking on tour, Sabrina returned in November 2018 with fresh music on *Singular: Act I*. This, more than ever before, was a record about an artist coming into her own. It was also the first time in her career that Sabrina had a hand in writing every single track on an album. As she told *W* magazine in 2018, "The concept that I found for this album later on was that I wasn't writing about confidence; I could just hear a new confidence embodied throughout it."

The lead single, "Almost Love," topped the Billboard Dance Club charts, and "Sue Me" soon followed to No. 1. The album stretches Sabrina even more stylistically, bringing in heavy influences of R&B and a variety of lush sonic landscapes, beginning with the heavy electronic beats in "Almost Love," continuing to the layered vocals of "Prfct," and ending with the swelling orchestral strains of "Diamonds Are Forever."

THE VIBE: A big dollop of R&B mixed with electropop makes for some danceable good fun.

CRITICAL RECEPTION: "Jam-packed with bop after bop...[and] lush with potential hits.... Another near-perfect work from one of the industry's brightest young stars."—*Idolator*

> Come and say, "Hi, I've been dying to meet ya"
> Don't leave me hanging like the Mona Lisa

WHEN YOU'RE UP: Dare you not to dance to "Almost Love," a song that sounds like Sabrina channeling the Caribbean vibes of Rihanna.

WHEN YOU'RE DOWN: "Diamonds Are Forever" is the song to get you back up on your feet. A send-up to slouches everywhere, this song is a sly anthem celebrating one's self-worth.

spotlight on STARGATE

Stargate is the moniker for the Norwegian dynamic duo Mikkel Eriksen and Tor Erik Hermansen. After achieving success in their home country (along with partner Hallgeir Rustan), the duo moved to the US, where they quickly gained traction with numerous pop artists, rising to such prominence that they've been dubbed the heir apparent to titanic R&B producers L.A. Reid and Babyface, and Jimmy Jam and Terry Lewis.

Certified hitmakers, Stargate is the producer behind such ubiquitous hits as Beyoncé's "Irreplaceable" and Rihanna's "Rude Boy," "Diamonds," and "Only Girl (In the World)," among many others. They also coproduced Coldplay's 2015 album *A Head Full of Dreams*. With juice like that, it's little wonder Sabrina wanted to collab. She cowrote "Almost Love" with Steph Jones, Nate Campany, and Stargate, who also produced the track.

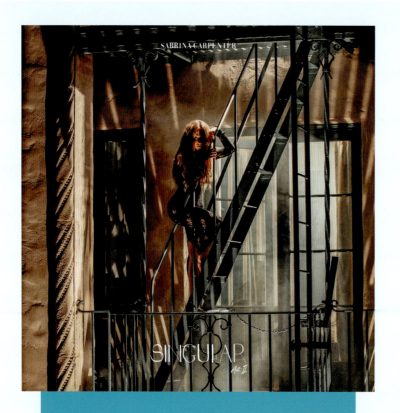

SINGULAR act II

Track List:

1. In My Bed
2. Pushing 20
3. I Can't Stop Me
4. I'm Fakin
5. Take Off All Your Cool
6. Tell Em
7. Exhale
8. Take You Back
9. Looking at Me

Singular Act II was released in July 2019. It would be the last of Sabrina's four albums with Hollywood Records. At 20 years old, she closed a long chapter in her career spent under the label's umbrella. On the album, she embraces a variety of musical genres, from electropop ("In My Bed") to trap ("Pushing 20") to Latin beats (the standout "Looking at Me").

The coda to *Singular* found her stretching her range more than ever before, earning her some of the most favorable reviews of her career to that point. "Very rarely is there an artist that can straddle, move between, and operate within, the areas of child star, pop star, and musical force," wrote *Paper* magazine. "Sabrina Carpenter...happens to be one of [them].... Each song on *Singular: Act II* draws on something different... [I]t's a culmination of pop eras—a rich plurality that separates itself from anything modern hit-writing has tried to glue together in recent years."

THE VIBE: All grown up, Sabrina takes on a harder edge in this collection of confident dance tracks.

CRITICAL RECEPTION: "Carpenter sings from her heart with an elevated maturity and honest vulnerability that makes this set very different [from] her last.... [It's] all about finding yourself through different life moments and coming to terms with who you are and who you want to be.... It's definitely an anthem for all the young people out there asking themselves the same questions as the pop singer, and that relatability is paramount in Carpenter's success."—*L'Officiel*

> *Think I'm reaching my limit*
> *Can I exhale for a minute?*

WHEN YOU'RE UP: The infectious R&B throwback "Pushing 20" is TLC's "No Scrubs" for the next generation.

WHEN YOU'RE DOWN: The soaring "Exhale" perfectly articulates the sense of being overwhelmed that comes with anxiety.

spotlight on SAWEETIE

Put two rising stars in the studio together, and sometimes you get brilliant results. That was the case with Sabrina and Saweetie, who appeared on the dreamy "I Can't Stop Me," cowritten by Sabrina and Stargate. Diamanté Harper, better known by her stage name, Saweetie, got her start as a rapper in the Bay Area, where she earned comparisons to such hip-hop titans as Lil' Kim. She broke out with her lead single "ICY GRL" in 2017, which went double platinum. Also known for her collaborations with Doja Cat, Migos' Quavo, and John Legend, among others, Saweetie remains an in-demand talent. She's also a highly sought-after marketer, with brand partnerships including McDonald's, True Religion, MAC Cosmetics, and Fenty.

"I've always been true to myself and believed in my work since I was young. I've realized that it's always been about the small baby steps that you take over time to get you to this point."

—Sabrina to *People*

BREAKING
through

STEPPING OUT of the Disney mold, Sabrina **COMES INTO HER OWN** as an artist.

The future's so bright, she's gotta wear shades.

After nearly 10 years and four albums, Sabrina left Disney's Hollywood Records for a new home at Island Records. It was a huge shift for the artist, who felt newly unencumbered to forge her own musical path wherever she pleased. Though she had established a solid bedrock in her career with her first label, she never felt she truly had creative freedom.

"For a long time, I was constantly guided and misguided," she told *Time*, looking back in 2024. "I'm so grateful for all of those times where I was led astray, because now I'm a lot more equipped going into situations where I have to trust my own instincts."

Sabrina's first effort with Island paid immediate dividends. Her first single released by her new label, "Skin," became her first single to chart on the Billboard Hot 100. Unfortunately, it didn't come without controversy, as many saw it as a response to Olivia Rodrigo's "drivers license." Is Sabrina the "blonde girl who always made me doubt," as the Rodrigo song goes? "Maybe 'blonde' was the only rhyme," Sabrina seemingly shot back in response. Rumors swirled that both songs addressed a love triangle with Joshua Bassett, who began dating Sabrina shortly after splitting with Rodrigo.

Sabrina's willingness to really go there—to reveal the parts of herself most people would keep hidden—is a hallmark

> **"I just adore Sabrina. And she's going to be around forever because she's such a great songwriter."**
>
> —hitmaker and producer Jack Antonoff, who collaborated with Sabrina on several *Short n' Sweet* tracks

of her songwriting. Pop music isn't just about shiny, happy, dance-y feelings. It can be about the uncomfortable stuff too. It's really about connecting with the listener and tapping into a vein that resonates with fans. "Everyone thinks of pop music as this really light, feathery type of thing that's supposed to make us bop through life like everything's fine," Sabrina said to *Paper* magazine. "I feel like I always was inspired to take things that I was going through that were more uncomfortable situations—not the brightest or the most positive—and musically shift the narrative. You end up remaking your memories as something that you can listen to, that doesn't remind you of a negative time."

All those difficult experiences—boy drama, girl drama, family drama—crystallized into the songs of *Emails I Can't Send*, Sabrina's first full album on her new label. Critics lavished praise on the album's "radical honesty" (*Vogue*), where "with one voice, millions feel heard" (*V* magazine). The record was also a commercial success, landing Sabrina her best sales numbers and chart history to that point.

The giant leap forward was no surprise to Eric Vetro, Sabrina's longtime vocal coach and a witness to her evolving career. He reflected, "Not only did she have a great voice for a 12-year-old, she also had an incredibly mature attitude about what she wanted to achieve in her career and how she was going to accomplish it," he told *Variety*. "I worried that she might burn out from starting so young, but those fears evaporated when I witnessed her working harder than ever year after year."

Indeed, Sabrina's work ethic is a vital key to her success as an artist, something that's been there since the very beginning. She remembers being sent to songwriting camps while with Disney. Ordinarily the artists would show up for a little face

With Antonoff in 2024.

SABRINA CARPENTER

time with the writers before making a quick exit—enough to give songwriters an idea of their personalities and the sorts of subjects that might suit them. They certainly weren't expected to drive the conversation or roll up their sleeves and start writing themselves. "They didn't realize I was the person that was gonna get there 30 minutes before everybody, and then not leave until an hour after, and be cutting vocals and backgrounds for hours. Whatever it takes," she told *Teen Vogue* in 2021.

Sabrina poured all of herself into *Emails*, and reaped the rewards of its success. Yet despite the upward trajectory she experienced with that record, there was nothing that could have prepared her for the seismic event that was *Short n' Sweet*. Straight out of the gates, the album was a sensation. It absolutely ruled the Billboard charts, besting Sabrina's previous marks and scoring her first No. 1 single when "Please Please Please" shot to the top of the pops. The second single, "Espresso," was the uncontested song of the summer and the most streamed song of the year by any artist. *Short n' Sweet* sold at a fever pitch, becoming the third-best-selling album of the year behind two musical titans; only Taylor Swift's *The Tortured Poets Department* and The Weeknd's *The Highlights* sold more copies in 2024.

And speaking of Swift, Sabrina joined the star for a huge swing on the massive Eras tour, where Sabrina played in front of the biggest crowds of her life. And soon after, Sabrina announced her own tour, selling out every date immediately.

Seemingly overnight, Sabrina mania was in full tilt. Suddenly everyone wanted

hold my gold

Ten years into her recording career, Sabrina finally struck gold with her sixth studio album. She took home two awards at the 67th Grammy Awards, held on February 2, 2025: Best Pop Vocal Album for *Short n' Sweet* and Best Pop Solo Performance for "Espresso."

Sabrina was awarded the ultimate validation when she won two Grammys for Short n' Sweet in 2025.

Carpenters have nothing but love for Sabrina, seen here performing at the 2023 Lollapalooza festival.

No Nonsense

to know everything about the singer. Gossip magazines followed her every move. Who was she dating? What was she wearing? Who were her songs written about? Fans turned into song detectives, decoding every lyric and picking apart every music video. For a singer who wore her heart on her sleeve, there wasn't a lot of mystery to uncover, but the attention was next-level.

Still, the cult of fascination with Sabrina wasn't about her celebrity at all. In fact, she was finally getting noticed for the thing that had always been there: her love of music and her commitment to the art form. Success is gratifying, sure, but you have to love the process, not just the results. "There are moments in everyone's life where the stars align," Sabrina told *Paper* in 2024. "But it wouldn't have happened if I hadn't spent the last years working so hard."

After a year filled with career superlatives, Sabrina capped *Short n' Sweet*'s incredible run with a rousing—and hilarious!—performance at the 2025 Grammys (another bucket list item) and took home two Grammy Awards for her work, her first ever. In a year jam-packed with milestone after milestone, that may have been the biggest of them all.

Following is a deep dive into Sabrina's Island Records albums *Emails I Can't Send* and *Short n' Sweet*.

SHORT N' SWEET *by the numbers*

- **2** Grammys
- **3** Billboard Top 10 singles
- **12** tracks on the album
- **12** Hot 100 singles
- **1+ million** in physical album sales
- **233 million** streams in its first week
- **5.5 billion** streams on Spotify worldwide

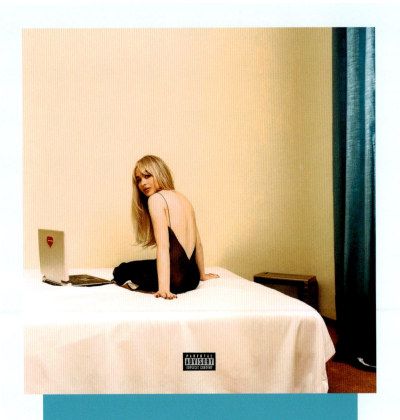

EMAILS *i can't* SEND

Track List:

1. Emails I Can't Send
2. Vicious
3. Read Your Mind
4. Tornado Warnings
5. Because I Liked a Boy
6. Already Over
7. How Many Things
8. Bet U Wanna
9. Nonsense
10. Fast Times
11. Skinny Dipping
12. Bad for Business
13. Decode

Sabrina's fifth album, released in July 2022, is organized around the titular idea of emails written but not sent—missives she wrote to herself as a form of catharsis during the COVID pandemic. The songs on the record express a range of emotions stemming from real-life events, including breakups, infidelity, and tabloid drama. The record represents a giant leap forward in Sabrina's musical evolution. Under her new label, she felt like she had a newfound independence where it came to charting her course. "This was finally the album where I got to just have fun," she told *Teen Vogue*. "It was completely and entirely just me steering the ship."

It was her best-selling album to that point, and it was also widely acclaimed. (*Rolling Stone* named it one of the 100 best albums of the year.) A deluxe version of the album, *Emails I Can't Send Fwd*, was released in March 2023; it contained four additional bonus tracks: "Opposite," "Lonesome," "Things I Wish You Said," and the breakout "Feather."

THE VIBE: Pure pop perfection, punctuated by moments of raw, elegant balladry.

CRITICAL RECEPTION: "Where *Emails I Can't Send* departs from Carpenter's heroes from decades past...is in its sprinkling of very Gen Z references (from unread texts to lying to your therapist to anonymous online death threats), among more timeless, heart-on-your-sleeve elegies to lost love. It feels like the most fully realized vision of Carpenter the musician—and the most rounded portrait of Carpenter the human being—yet."—*Vogue*

> *I wonder how many things you think about before you get to me*

WHEN YOU'RE UP: Sabrina's perfect description of getting tongue-tied by falling in love at first sight made "Nonsense" an instant fan favorite.

WHEN YOU'RE DOWN: With lyrics like "You were all I looked up to / Now I can't even look at you," "Emails I Can't Send" perfectly channels the waves of fury that can come with a bad breakup.

spotlight on
JULIA MICHAELS AND JP SAXE

Sabrina described them as her "musical mom and dad," and collaborators Julia Michaels and JP Saxe made magic with Sabrina on this record, contributing to nearly every single.

Michaels is a multi-Grammy-nominated songwriter who has worked with pop's biggest names—everyone from Justin Bieber and Britney Spears to Olivia Rodrigo and Selena Gomez—over the last two decades. She is also a performer in her own right. Saxe, a Canadian singer-songwriter, has released two studio albums with Arista and has been a featured artist with numerous other groups. Also a prolific writer, he's penned songs for Ariana DeBose, Lewis Capaldi, and Gayle, among others.

Together, Saxe and Michaels cowrote and recorded the devastating ballad "If the World Was Ending," which was released in 2019 and became a runaway hit during the early days of COVID isolation. Their musical chemistry bled into real life, and they got together as a couple soon after. (They have since broken up.)

SHORT n' SWEET

Track List:

1. Taste
2. Please Please Please
3. Good Graces
4. Sharpest Tool
5. Coincidence
6. Bed Chem
7. Espresso
8. Dumb & Poetic
9. Slim Pickins
10. Juno
11. Lie to Girls
12. Don't Smile

Describing the record as the "hot older sister" of *Emails I Can't Send*, Sabrina continued her genre-mixing ways in this, her sixth album. "Please Please Please" recalls a disco-era Dolly Parton and "Bed Chem" and "Good Graces" echo vintage Ariana Grande, while songs like "Slim Pickins" give a Kacey Musgraves vibe. The throughline that holds it all together is the tone, which is equal parts caustic, cheeky, and self-aware—in short, what makes Sabrina, Sabrina.

Short n' Sweet hit shelves on August 23, 2024, at the tail end of what tourmate Taylor Swift called "the summer of Sabrina." There are hardly enough superlatives to describe the album's reception. Both singles launched before the album's release—"Please Please Please" and "Espresso"—became runaway hits and launched Sabrina into a different stratosphere. The album shattered sales records, gained widespread critical attention, and spawned countless cover stories and think pieces. It was nominated for six Grammys, winning two.

THE VIBE: As country singer Martina McBride once famously intoned, this one's for the girls. *Short n' Sweet* is filled with bop after bop after vicious, funny, fabulous bop.

CRITICAL RECEPTION: "Who Sabrina Carpenter is has never been clearer—and her long-awaited, hard-earned climb to pop's summit should continue with ease."—*NME*

> *You don't have to lie to girls*
> *If they like you, they'll just lie to themselves*
> *Like you, they'll just lie to themselves*

WHEN YOU'RE UP: The world's still wired on Sabrina's "me espresso," from the undisputed song of the year!

WHEN YOU'RE DOWN: Whether or not it's about a certain Canadian pop star, "Sharpest Tool" explores the universal feelings of being dumped.

spotlight on AMY ALLEN

Allen is one of the most sought-after songwriters in the industry, a talent who's had a hand in some of the biggest albums of the past decade. She was nominated for the first-ever Songwriter of the Year Grammy for her work in 2022 with artists Charli XCX, Lizzo, King Princess, and Harry Styles (among many others), and she took a Grammy for Album of the Year for Styles's *Harry's House* that year.

In the last year alone, Allen has cranked out some of the year's biggest smashes, from Tate McRae's "Greedy" to Justin Timberlake's "Selfish" and Rosé and Bruno Mars's "Apt." As *New York Times* music writer Joe Coscarelli put it, "Top 40, in no small part thanks to Allen, is entering a much-needed era of quirk, in which regular jolts of the unexpected are cutting through a sludge of smooth-brained content."

Allen is also a performer in her own right, an indie singer-songwriter whose '90s-inflected music recalls artists such as Edie Brickell, Alanis Morissette, and their forebears, such as Joni Mitchell.

"I had a lot of ideas musically, and for the one thing that pulls it all together to be my point of view. That was the one thing that I knew.... [G]rowing up [I had] a lot of people telling me: You have to stay in your lane and pick your genre, otherwise you're not a cohesive artist and you don't know who you are. And that always bugged me."

—Sabrina on *Short n' Sweet* to *Vogue* in 2025

6

BORN *to* PERFORM

*From the **SMALL SCREEN** to the world's biggest arenas, **ALL THE WORLD'S A STAGE** for Sabrina.*

Performing for fans in Atlanta during the 2023 iHeartRadio Jingle Ball.

Sabrina has been playing to crowds her whole life, from her earliest days in Pennsylvania. She's a tireless performer who feeds off the energy of the crowd. She loves live performances because each show feels unique. "Every performance is different, based off how the audience is feeling and what they're giving me," she told *Vogue* in 2024. That kind of variation is what exhilarates her and drives her desire to share her music with fans.

In 2020, she took on a new frontier as a live performer, playing Cady Heron in the highly touted musical adaption of *Mean Girls* on Broadway. It was her first Broadway production and a major stepping stone in an acting career beyond Disney. The role was tailor-made for Sabrina, who's a triple threat as a singer, actor, and dancer. She rehearsed the production for months on end, and then, only two performances into its run, the play was shuttered as all the lights on the Great White Way went dark for COVID precautions. "[That] humbled me very quickly," Sabrina told *CBS Sunday Morning*. "I was sent home and just was like, 'Wow. I feel like I could do eight shows a week, you know, and I've been training for it, and now it's just silence.'"

It turns out that isolation was a blessing in disguise, as Sabrina was able to channel her emotions and vulnerabilities into the songs that

SABRINA CARPENTER

became the tracks on *Emails I Can't Send*. In 2023, Sabrina announced her upcoming tour in support of the record, and the response was overwhelming. The tour sold out all of its dates immediately.

"Touring is never easy, I'm pretty honest about that, but it was such a gift. This tour has been so much more fun than any other show I've ever put on," she told *Vogue* of the experience.

It was also on that tour that she started what became one of her most beloved traditions. Fans were on the edge of their seats waiting to hear what salacious verse she'd ad-lib at the end of her "Nonsense" performances.

And when she got the call to join Taylor Swift on the Eras tour, it was a tradition she brought with her. Opening for Swift, arguably the biggest pop star in the world, was intimidating, but it was also exhilarating. Not only was Sabrina playing for massive crowds in some of the world's biggest arenas, but she was also doing it basically alone. She had no sets, no props, no backup dancers— it was just her and her music, reaching the masses.

Sabrina first met Swift in 2017. The superstar was backstage with her cats, and the two bonded over their affinity for felines. But when the call came from the Swift camp in 2024, Sabrina was floored. "Still trying to process, but I shan't," she told her Instagram followers when the announcement went out.

The Eras tour solidified a friendship between the two performers, something Sabrina often describes as a big sister / little sister dynamic. "To work with someone [who] cares about you as a person as well as

Good Tines!

A nod to the lyrics in "How Many Things"—in which seeing a fork stirs a haunting memory of an ex-boyfriend—Sabrina's fans raise the utensil at her shows in tribute.

Taylor Swift has a knack for picking talented tourmates. Among her opening acts who have gone on to lucrative careers are Ed Sheeran, Phoebe Bridgers, Charli XCX, Camila Cabello, and Shawn Mendes.

Performing on the Short n' Sweet tour in New York City.

No Nonsense

> **"I never would have expected that going on a tour would have amplified the songs the way that it did. And I just feel lucky that people have found them in different places and now see them in different lights."**
>
> —Sabrina to *Variety*

an artist…that's been the biggest gift for sure," Sabrina told Who What Wear.

Sabrina also learned plenty from Swift about anchoring a giant stage show. Swift's innovation, discipline, and generosity all left a big impression on her. "I feel so lucky to witness the magic that is you and this tour," she wrote to Taylor via Instagram in 2024. "there is truly no one like you and there never will be! i love you with all my heart and i will cherish this taybrina era (and all the eras) till the end of time."

It was on tour with Taylor when Sabrina started writing songs that would become *Short n' Sweet*. In between tour dates on Eras, Sabrina took 10 days in a small town in France, where she began work on songs for the album. It was in a café sipping, yes, espresso where she came up with the kernel for what would become a smash hit. She wrote the rest of the album with collaborators at the iconic Electric Lady Studios in New York, where some of rock 'n' roll's most enduring albums were recorded.

And when the time came to tour *Short n' Sweet*, Carpenters were ready. The tour sold out immediately (again), and she was set to play some of the biggest arenas in the country and abroad. A far cry from the stripped-down staging for her set on the Eras tour, the ongoing Short n' Sweet tour doesn't skimp on spectacle. The show is structured in three acts, each with its own distinct sets and costumes. Sabrina is supported by a chorus line of backup dancers who swan around the star. The whole thing has a decidedly throwback feel to it, as if she's the leading lady in a classic Hollywood musical. The backdrop is a stylized penthouse apartment that looks like it was lifted straight out of an old movie, and Sabrina moves seamlessly through the rooms as she performs. The whole affair sparkles with a uniquely retro effervescence.

Gone are the revolving outros from "Nonsense," but there is an interactive element that makes each show its

On the Singular tour in 2019.

own. Each night she performs a unique cover song by spinning a bottle onstage, a sort of karaoke roulette. Among the songs included in the mix: ABBA's "Mamma Mia," Sixpence None the Richer's "Kiss Me," *Grease*'s "Hopelessly Devoted to You," Dolly Parton's "9 to 5," and even Rick James's "Super Freak."

Suffice it to say, Sabrina owns the spotlight no matter what the night brings her, and her newest tour is the most ambitious and assured to date. For this, she credits her fans. "I don't take any of you for granted and I'm so appreciative of the way you show your love and express it," she wrote to them via email at the end of the year.

If you missed Sabrina on this tour, don't fret. It's only a matter of time before she's back on a stage near you. "I will tour until I die, probably," she told *Paper* magazine. "It's a huge part of my life. In a weird way, it helps me move on to the next chapter, mentally. I feel like every time I've been able to write a record and perform it, I'm able to set it free."

And it's only a matter of time before Sabrina is on to the next. "I'm always sort of thinking one year ahead," she told *The Hollywood Reporter*. "I've started thinking about what will come after *Short n' Sweet*, but for now I'm just letting myself grow and have fun with it." Whenever that next chapter comes, Carpenters are here for it!

FAN *fare*

Superstars Selena Gomez, Cardi B, and Adele are among Sabrina's multitude of fans. Her concerts are star-studded events, attended by the likes of Cara Delevingne, Kendall Jenner, Hailey Bieber, Miranda Cosgrove, Madison Beer, John Mayer, Jessica Alba, Ben Platt, Lance Bass, and so many more. Here are just a few of the many superlatives that have been lavished upon Sabrina by her celeb stans.

"[The] pop princess of our dreams."
—Taylor Swift

"She's lovely…. I love seeing pop girls win, always."
—Chappell Roan

"We're little, we're blonde, and we love each other."
—Dolly Parton

"An incredible talent who is absolutely smashing it."
—Elton John

"That song ['Espresso'] is my jam!"
—Adele

"I'm so happy for [Sabrina and Chappell Roan]. It's a crazy world when you get to the level they're experiencing right now, and they're doing great. Fans are drawn to them because they're…awesome."
—Billie Eilish

"I was always in love with her voice…. There's something about certain voices, like all of the greatest voices, you just stop even thinking about what's happening and you're like, 'Oh, it's always existed.' There's not a lot of those voices. So when you hear one, you never forget it."
—Jack Antonoff

"Sabrina Carpenter's new album is such a pop album, but then there's little country moments…. It's great. What are we supposed to do, rediagnose that? No…. It's all rock 'n' roll, baby."
—Finneas

"I love her. I love the whole batch of young [female artists] that are so loud and proud and unapologetic."
—Katy Perry

Fangirling backstage with Katy Perry at the 2024 MTV Video Music Awards.

Sabrina in 2016.

WHAT'S *in a* NAME

Sabrina shares quite a bit in common with her name twins. As the song goes, what a coincidence! (Or is it?)

Famous Sabrinas

Sabrina Spellman: Better known as Marvel Comics' Sabrina the Teenage Witch, the headstrong teenager has been played on-screen by Melissa Joan Hart and Kiernan Shipka.

Sabrina Bryan: Best known for her role in Disney's *The Cheetah Girls*, the blonde with the big voice shares a few key attributes with Sabrina Carpenter.

Sabrina Duncan: When it comes to girl power, is there anything more iconic than *Charlie's Angels*? One of the OG Angels, she was played on TV by Kate Jackson.

Famous Carpenters

Karen Carpenter: Sabrina grew up listening to the Carpenters, a big early influence. Karen was known for her soulful, powerful voice and mastery of singing with emotion. Bonus: she was also an awesome drummer!

John Carpenter: The visionary film director is the mind behind classic movies such as *Halloween*. He is also a talented musician who scored many of his movies.

Mary Chapin Carpenter: This singer-songwriter has won five Grammy Awards in her long recording career.

Short n' Sweet Goes Live

Sabrina hit the road, playing date after sold-out date in the fall of 2024 in promotion of her new album. Then in early 2025 she started a European tour, crisscrossing the continent. Were you one of the lucky Carpenters who got to see her?

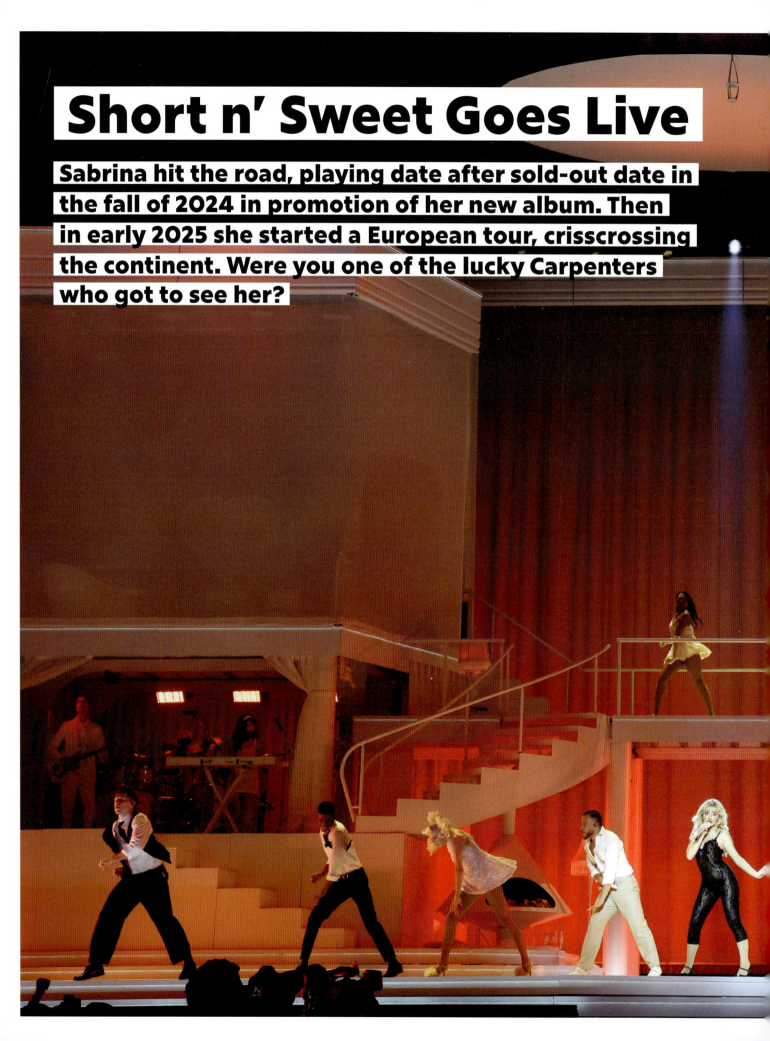

September 23, 2024	Columbus, OH	November 4, 2024	Vancouver, BC
September 25, 2024	Toronto, ON	November 6, 2024	Seattle, WA
September 26, 2024	Detroit, MI	November 7, 2024	Portland, OR
September 29, 2024	New York, NY	November 9, 2024	San Francisco, CA
September 30, 2024	Brooklyn, NY	November 10, 2024	San Diego, CA
October 2, 2024	Hartford, CT	November 13, 2024	Phoenix, AZ
October 3, 2024	Boston, MA	November 15, 2024	Los Angeles, CA
October 5, 2024	Baltimore, MD	November 17-18, 2024	Inglewood, CA
October 8, 2024	Philadelphia, PA	March 3-4, 2025	Dublin, Ireland
October 11, 2024	Montreal, QC	March 6, 2025	Birmingham, England
October 13, 2024	Chicago, IL	March 8-9, 2025	London, England
October 14, 2024	Minneapolis, MN	March 11, 2025	Glasgow, Scotland
October 16, 2024	Nashville, TN	March 13-14, 2025	Manchester, England
October 17, 2024	St. Louis, MO	March 16-17, 2025	Paris, France
October 19, 2024	Raleigh, NC	March 19, 2025	Berlin, Germany
October 20, 2024	Charlottesville, VA	March 22, 2025	Brussels, Belgium
October 22, 2024	Atlanta, GA	March 23, 2025	Amsterdam, Netherlands
October 24, 2024	Orlando, FL	March 26, 2025	Milan, Italy
October 25, 2024	Tampa, FL	March 27, 2025	Zürich, Switzerland
October 27, 2024	Houston, TX	March 30, 2025	Oslo, Norway
October 28, 2024	Austin, TX	March 31-April 1, 2025	Copenhagen, Denmark
October 30, 2024	Dallas, TX	April 3-4, 2025	Stockholm, Sweden
November 1, 2024	Denver, CO	July 5, 2025	London, England
November 2, 2024	Salt Lake City, UT		

7

all that GLITTERS

This chapter celebrates **SABRINA'S PASSION FOR FASHION,** *proving she has style for miles!*

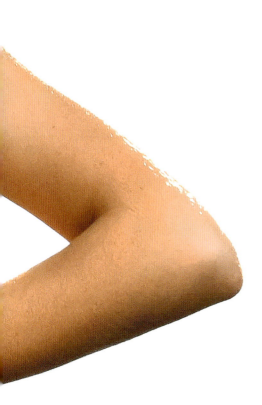

Wearing FROLOV onstage at the 2024 Governors Ball in New York.

As you might expect from someone who's been in the business as long as Sabrina has, she's walked her fair share of red carpets. But Sabrina's mastery of the *lewk* goes far beyond the old adage of practice, practice, practice. She's got a signature style that absolutely slays.

First and foremost, it starts with the beauty look. "My mom introduced makeup to my sisters and [me] at a very young age because we were dancers.... I just learned a lot of lessons about makeup from a young age," she told *Elle*. Having that extra time to experiment with cosmetics informed her approach: less is always more.

Sabrina's secret to a good face is great skincare—she has a pretty strict regimen. And after years of wearing stage makeup on set, she's found that she prefers the natural look. On a typical day, she'll do a simple routine. She plays up her prominent cheekbones with contouring and highlighter. Her strong brows are a defining feature, and she usually finishes with a neutral lip. Of course, she leaves plenty of room for play: "One of the coolest things about makeup is you can... really just do whatever feels right for you that day," she said.

Sabrina's long, blonde locks have been a mainstay for her entire career, and one of the pillars of her signature look. In 2024 she partnered with hair care brand

Redken, becoming its first-ever global ambassador. The team-up with Redken is one of many brand sponsorships the starlet has inked already. She's been featured in campaigns for Converse and Aéropostale, and was the face of a campaign for Kim Kardashian's SKIMS; she's also represented high-end brands including Versace and Marc Jacobs.

Sabrina tapped the Ukrainian brand FROLOV for an onstage look for her Emails I Can't Send tour, helping to amplify the brand's reach in the US. The heart-cutout dresses she's worn from the designer are among her most iconic looks.

Sabrina loves to experiment with her clothes, but if there's one mainstay, it has to be Versace. "For as long as I can remember, I've been a fan of Versace and Donatella, and the way they make women feel in the clothes," she told *Vogue*. "I write my songs from that perspective, and I try to live every day with that kind of confidence."

That kind of confidence is no small feat, considering that the 5'0" star is often in towering shoes. She was six or seven the first time she put on high heels, and started wearing them regularly as a young teen. "My feet, somehow, are doing fine," she quipped to Lynn Hirschberg in 2024.

Sabrina's small stature also poses challenges when it comes to clothing. "I'm very petite, so a lot of the time, fashion for me is more than just a beautiful dress—it's the way that it lays on you, and accentuates you," she told *Vogue*.

Sabrina doesn't have a dedicated stylist, but she has worked with a few heavy hitters on her music videos and tours. Ronnie Hart created the looks for the iconic *Short n' Sweet* videos "Please Please Please," "Espresso," and "Taste"— an eclectic mix of retro-inspired looks and vampy dresses befitting a femme fatale. He also styled her for "Feather," "Because I Liked a Boy," and "Nonsense," from her previous album, *Emails I Can't*

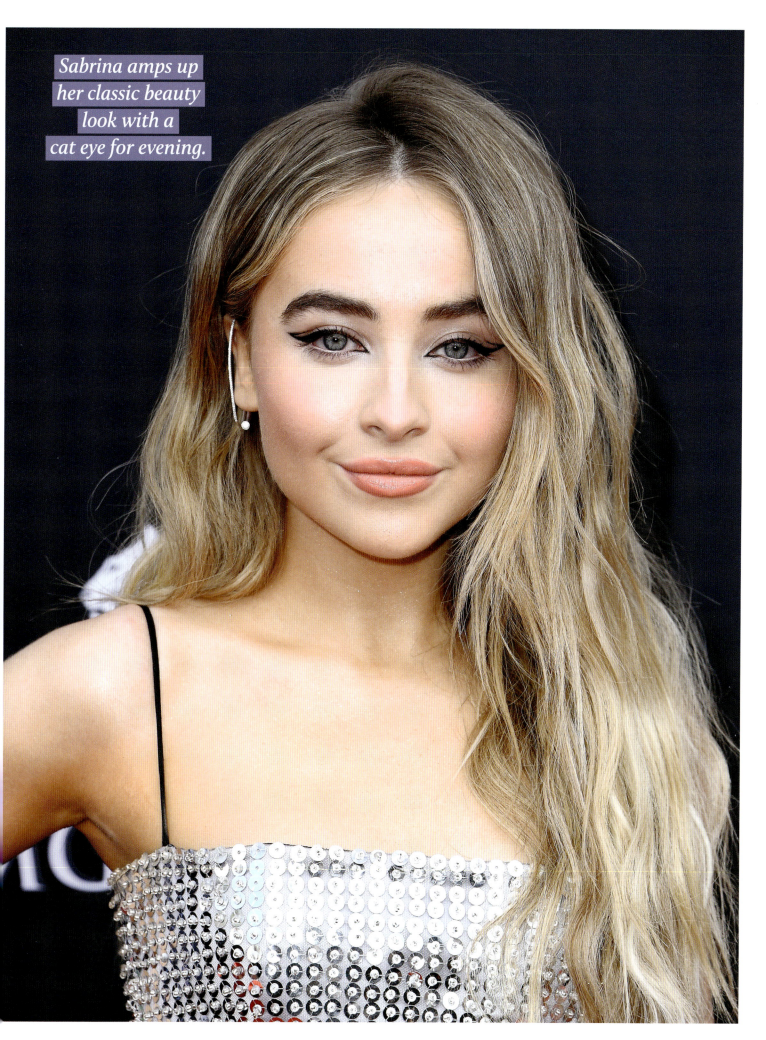

Sabrina amps up her classic beauty look with a cat eye for evening.

Sabrina has been a muse for designers Marc Jacobs and Donatella Versace, among others.

No Nonsense

"I can't resist the sparkles."
—Sabrina to *W* magazine

Send. "He has such a great eye when it comes to seeing something that is modern and timeless at the same time," Sabrina told *Vogue*.

Hart's playful sensibility is a perfect match for Sabrina, whose self-described twisted sense of humor is often on display. "No matter what I do, I always try to have a sense of levity and remember that fashion is meant to be fun," Hart said to *Paper* magazine.

Jared Ellner, who styles celebs including Emma Chamberlain and Rachel Sennott, created the lingerie-inspired looks for Sabrina's *Short n' Sweet* rollout, which channeled the classic pinup style of icons including Marilyn Monroe and Madonna. In addition to commissioning new pieces for some of her onstage looks, he pulled several from the Victoria's Secret archives and other vintage vaults.

Sabrina's provocative way of dressing has drawn criticism from some parents, but she has come to terms with that; she knows it's not for everyone, and that's okay.

"The scariest thing in the world is getting up on a stage in front of that many people and having to perform as if it's nothing," she told *Time*. "If the one thing that helps you do that is the way you feel comfortable dressing, then that's what you've got to do."

Like anyone else, her sense of style has transformed over time. "The things I feel really confident in now, maybe five years ago I probably would have never worn [them], but that's the beautiful thing about evolving with fashion," she told Who What Wear. "I'm constantly exploring and figuring [things] out."

On the street, you might see Sabrina in sporty silhouettes, such as crop tops and baggy pants, or teeny skirts and big jackets—it's all about contrast. On the red carpet, she favors bombshell glamour: sculpted silhouettes, cutouts, and lots of glitz. She's sported so many fabulous looks over the years, it's hard to winnow them down to the best of the best. But here are 10 of Sabrina's most successful fashion moments to date.

10 BEST LOOKS

10 IN MARC JACOBS; 2017

9
IN CUSTOM PATOU: 2024

This is one of three bespoke outfits she wears onstage on her Short n' Sweet tour.

8
IN MÔNOT: 2022

7
IN VERSACE; 2018

6
IN ALICE + OLIVIA; 2016

5

IN CUSTOM PACO RABANNE; 2022

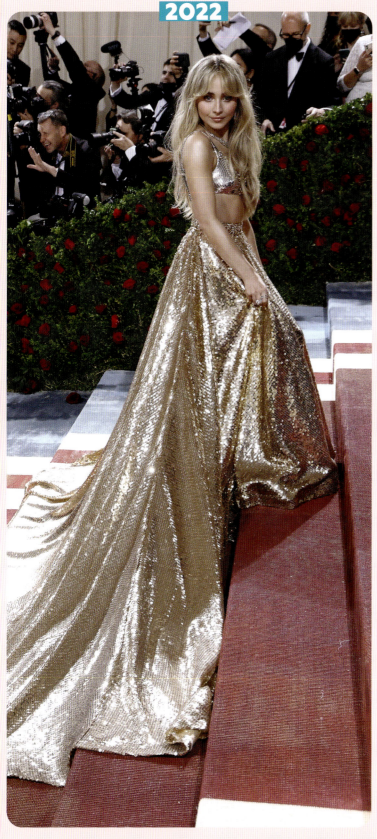

4

IN BOB MACKIE; 2024

This look was originally worn by Madonna at the 1991 Oscars!

3
IN MOSCHINO; 2022

2
IN ALBERTA FERRETTI; 2022

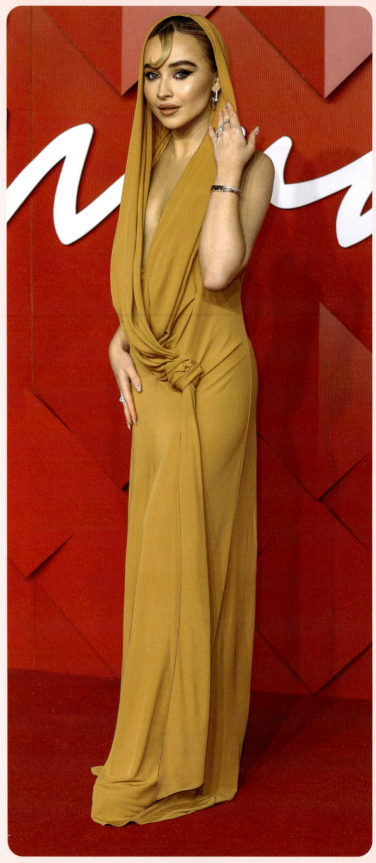

1
IN TORY BURCH; 2024

The custom-made dress featured a crocodile-print embossed bodysuit and a sheer, sequined silk chiffon skirt.

SABRINA from A to Z

A — *Alice's Adventures in Wonderland.* Her favorite book; her fans often bring her Alice-themed gifts.

B — Beatles. Her first musical love and a main songwriting influence.

C — Carpenters. The name of Sabrina's fan base.

D — Disney. Where it all began.

E — "Espresso." The ultra-catchy song catapulted her to next-level status!

F — "Feather." The bouncy single from *Emails I Can't Send* (2022) was her first Top 40 hit, reaching its pinnacle in 2023.

G — Grammy. Sabrina won her first Grammy Awards in 2025.

H — Hollywood. Not only was this the city she was destined to rule, but it was also the name of the record label that produced her first four albums.

I — Iced Coffee. Sabrina partnered with Dunkin' Donuts to release a special drink called Sabrina's Brown Sugar Shakin' Espresso in 2025.

J — Joey. Her BFF, Joey King.

K — Kiss. The lipstick mark is a major motif in her breakthrough album, *Short n' Sweet*.

L — Lucky. Her prized teddy bear; she even has his name tattooed behind her ear.

M — Maya Hart. Sabrina's *Girl Meets World* role.

N — "Nonsense." Sabrina switched the lyrics in this outro for every performance on her 2023 tour.

O — Opening Act. She joined childhood idols Ariana Grande and Taylor Swift on the artists' tours.

P — "Please Please Please." Her first No. 1 single.

Q Quakertown. The Pennsylvania town where Sabrina was born.

R Rihanna. A musical influence and all-around icon; Sabrina walked in her Savage x Fenty show in 2021.

S Sister. She's super-close with her three sibs.

T "Thumbs." One of Sabrina's earliest hits, it reached the top spot on Billboard's Bubbling Under Hot 100 chart.

U Ukulele. Sabrina plays the instrument, along with piano, guitar, bass, and a little bit of drums and harmonica.

V Variety. On her Short n' Sweet tour, Sabrina randomly selects which cover song she sings that night.

W Wordplay. Her love of language and clever wordplay is evident in her lyrics.

X Xtina. Christina Aguilera was a huge early influence.

Y YouTube. Sabrina started posting videos on the streaming site when she was 10.

Z Zac Efron. Her childhood crush!

GAME on

Think you know Sabrina?
TEST YOUR KNOWLEDGE *with the following quizzes and games to confirm if you're a* **TRUE CARPENTER!**

the WRITE stuff

Sabrina's songwriting talent is stellar. But how well do you know her words? Match the lyrics below to the songs in which they appear.

1. Oh I make quite an impression
   Five feet, to be exact.
2. If you don't want to cry to my music don't make me hate you prolifically.
3. Said you're not in my time zone but you wanna be.
4. That's my shape, I made the shadow
   That's my name. Don't wear it out, though.
5. That's just the way of the world
   It never ends till it ends, then it starts again.
6. And all of this for what?
   When everything went down, we were already broken up.
7. There's red and green everywhere, but I'm so blue.
8. We're never gonna turn to dust
   All we really need is us.

A. "Because I Liked a Boy"
B. "Bed Chem"
C. "Cindy Lou Who"
D. "Please Please Please"
E. "Sue Me"
F. "Taste"
G. "Thumbs"
H. "We'll Be the Stars"

The songwriter is never far away from a pen.

These two together are a force to be reckoned with.

WHO am I?

Sabrina has had some killer collabs over the course of her career, from her Disney-era singles with Sofia Carson to her recent duet with childhood idol Shania Twain. Can you identify her mystery collaborators from the following clues?

Known for my outspokenness and wild stage looks, Sabrina and I recorded a fun and flirty version of Wham's "Last Christmas" together.

Who am I?

Sabrina lent me her vocals and her acting chops, playing my girlfriend in the short film for my song "That's Not How This Works."

Who am I?

My collaboration with Sabrina on my song "Alien" helped her achieve her first No. 1 song on the Billboard Dance Club Songs chart.

Who am I?

Sabrina and I performed my songs "White Horse" and "Coney Island" onstage in front of more than 80,000 fans.

Who am I?

I was cast as Sabrina's nemesis in the video "Taste." But don't let the creepy (or kooky, mysterious, and ooky) exterior fool you—she and I are old friends.

Who am I?

FACT or FICTION

1. Sabrina has two cats, whom she named after members of the disco band the Bee Gees.
2. She often says that Beyoncé's *Lemonade* is her favorite album.
3. It was Sabrina's idea to release "Espresso" as a single; no one else at her label thought it was a single.
4. Her dog, Goodwin, is a purebred bichon frise.
5. Her grandmother was a dancer.
6. Her favorite place is France.
7. She released a Christmas EP called *Fruitcake*.
8. Sabrina's favorite food is steak fajitas.
9. Her childhood nickname was Little Singer Girl.
10. Other than hay fever, she does not have any allergies.
11. She played a supporting role in a Harry Potter movie.
12. She has a tattoo inspired by singer Etta James.
13. Her favorite color is pink.
14. Her BFF is actress Joey King.
15. Sabrina played *Mean Girls* character Regina George on Broadway.
16. Her first film role was in the Daniel Radcliffe movie *Horns*.
17. Her astrological sign is Libra.
18. Sports fans believe that Sabrina Carpenter's outfit choices during her tour stops have jinxed their teams.
19. Her favorite hobby is drawing.
20. Sabrina is set to star in a live-action film about Bratz dolls.

It's all about the fans.

Sabrina attends the Teen Choice Awards After Party with a Cause in 2013.

TIMELINE *challenge*

Put these singles in chronological order by release date, starting with her earliest.

"A Nonsense Christmas"

"Because I Liked a Boy"

"Can't Blame a Girl for Trying"

"Espresso"

"Feather"

"Please Please Please"

"Skinny Dipping"

"Thumbs"

MAD scramble

Sabrina has played so many memorable roles on TV and film over the years, from family comedies to serious dramas. How well do you know her list of screen credits? Unscramble each line to identify a different production starring Sabrina. Then rearrange the circled letters to answer the question below.

LIRG ESTEM DWROL

SCULDO

VARTDESUNE NI NIBGYTBISAT

NORSH

HET EATH U VIEG

LALT LIGR

GREMEYENC

MOIL SMYHUPR AWL

What's the best way to describe Sabrina's acting career?

__ __ __ __ ' __   " __ __ __   __ __ __ __ "

With on-screen sister Ava Michelle at the 2019 Tall Girl premiere.

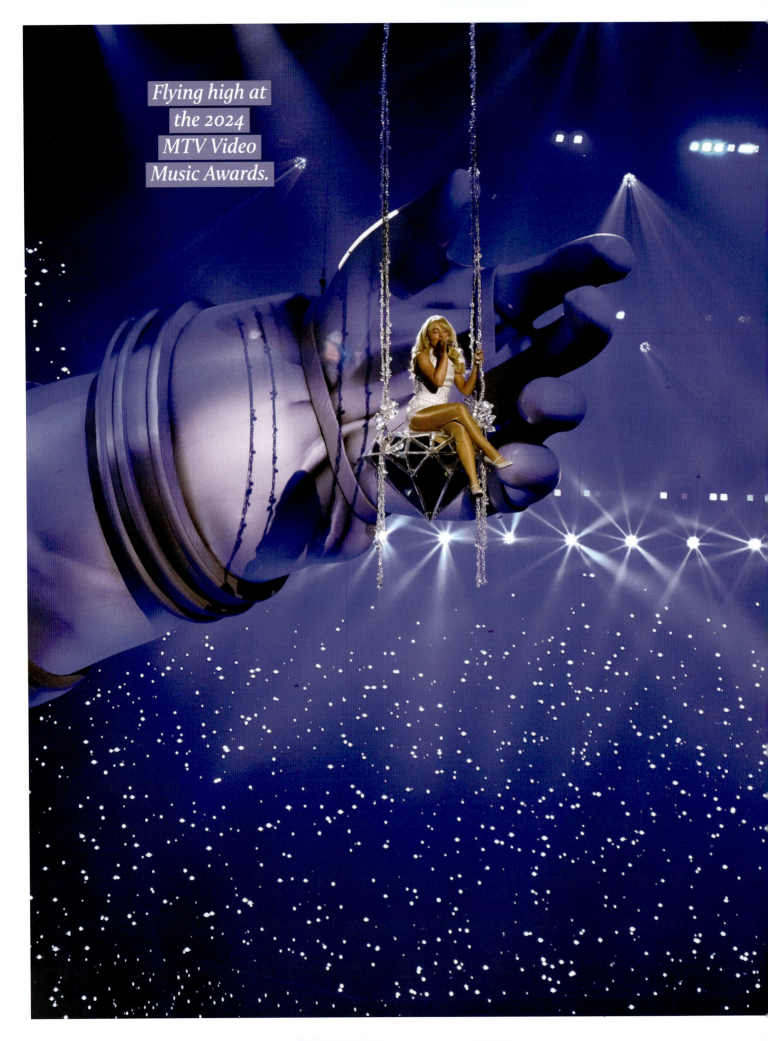

Flying high at the 2024 MTV Video Music Awards.

VIDEO *games*

Can you identify the videos from the descriptions below?

1. Two rivals after the same guy embark on a *Death Becomes Her*-esque revenge spree.

2. Jaded commuters shake off the monotony with a spirited subway dance-off.

3. Scores of guys prove they'd quite literally die to be with Sabrina.

4. Bad boyfriends only get so many second chances before they get cut loose (or in this case, turned in to law enforcement).

5. A slick special agent kicks butt and saves the day in this spy-themed vid.

6. Sabrina wants to hang out on the beach, not answer his calls.

7. Sabrina's kiss literally turns a boy to stone—yikes!

8. Channeling *Legally Blonde*'s Elle Woods, Sabrina pleads her case in a court of law.

Sabrina with Billie Eilish and Chappell Roan at the 2025 Grammy Awards.

Answers:

The Write Stuff: 1F, 2D, 3B, 4E, 5G, 6A, 7C, 8H.

Who Am I?: 1. Chappell Roan; 2. Charlie Puth; 3. Jonas Blue; 4. Taylor Swift; 5. Jenna Ortega.

Fact or Fiction: 1. False. They're named after Benny Andersson and Bjorn Ulvaeus of the disco band ABBA. 2. True. 3. True. 4. False. Goodwin is a mutt—part Maltese, Lhasa apso, and Chihuahua. 5. False. Her mother was a dancer and her grandmother was an artist. 6. True. 7. True. 8. False. It's chicken fajitas. 9. True. 10. False. She is allergic to almonds, apples, and grass, among other things. 11. False. But she is a certified Potterhead. 12. True. She has a tattoo that reads "At Last," after James's inspiring song, among her five tattoos. 13. False. It's yellow. 14. True. 15. False. She played Cady Heron in the production. 16. False. It was the 2012 comedy *Noobz*, starring Jason Mewes and Casper Van Dien. 17. False. A big believer in astrology, she believes to have many of the qualities of her sun sign, Taurus. 18. True. Google "Sabrina Carpenter Curse" and check out the silly superstition for yourself! 19. True. 20. False.

Timeline Challenge: "Can't Blame a Girl for Trying" (3/14/14); "Thumbs" (10/7/16); "Skinny Dipping" (9/9/21); "Because I Liked a Boy" (7/15/22); "A Nonsense Christmas" (12/7/22); "Feather" (3/17/23); "Espresso" (4/11/24); "Please Please Please" (6/6/24).

Mad Scramble: *Girl Meets World*; *Clouds*; *Adventures in Babysitting*; *Horns*; *The Hate U Give*; *Tall Girl*; *Emergency*; *Milo Murphy's Law*. A: SHE'S ON A "ROLE"

Video Games: 1. "Taste"; 2. "Thumbs"; 3. "Feather"; 4. "Please Please Please"; 5. "Fast Times"; 6. "Espresso"; 7. "Almost Love"; 8. "Sue Me."

"The music was always my life, and still is. I get so excited about things that move me, things that excite me. Being able to capture feelings into words and into melodies."